Mark Making

poems by

David McElroy

Finishing Line Press
Georgetown, Kentucky

Mark Making

Copyright © 2016 by David McElroy
ISBN 978-1-63534-062-4 First Edition
All rights reserved under International and Pan-American Copyright Conventions. No part of this book may be reproduced in any manner whatsoever without written permission from the publisher, except in the case of brief quotations embodied in critical articles and reviews.

ACKNOWLEDGMENTS

The following poems have appeared in these magazines:

Anchorage Daily News - "Palimpsest."
Great River Review – "Toolkit."
Blue Collar Review – "Trouble Shooter," and "Woman Reading, Dreaming."
Hearse - "Before Breakup on the Chena outside Fairbanks."
Ice-floe - "Andante," "Mark Making," "Breathing," and "My Life."
Iowa Review - "Getting a Drunk out of the Cab" and "The Woman in the Big Boy Restaurant and I."
Jeopardy - "Peanut Gallery."
Ohio Review - "What Makes Me Miss You."
Pacific Poetry and Fiction Review - "Looking for our Own Beauty."
Poetry Northwest - "For Kevin."

And the anthologies:
Finding the Boundaries - "Our Bodies in Bed," "Snorkeling with Lou Barr," and "Moving Train to Cactus Transfer."
Inroads - "-10," "Chiaroscuro," "My Life," "Round," and "Skiing with Brandon."
Poetspeak - "Before Breakup on the Chena Outside Fairbanks" and "Nocturne at the Institute."
Where We Are - "The Grandmother Factor."

I would like to thank the National Endowment for the Arts and the Alaska State Council on the Arts for their generous grants.

Publisher: Leah Maines
Editor: Christen Kincaid
Cover Art: Edith Barrowclough
Author Photo: Edith Barrowclough
Cover Design: Elizabeth Maines

Printed in the USA on acid-free paper.
Order online: www.finishinglinepress.com
                   also available on amazon.com

          Author inquiries and mail orders:
                Finishing Line Press
                  P. O. Box 1626
             Georgetown, Kentucky 40324
                     U. S. A.

Table of Contents

Andante

Andante 1
Round..3
My Life 4
Before Breakup on the Chena Outside Fairbanks......................5
Toolkit 6
Nervous Breakdown at Neah Bay...7
Balkan Cleansing..8
Nocturne..10

Surviving Winter

What Makes Me Miss you...12
-10..13
Moving Train to Cactus Transfer 14
Woman in the Big Boy Restaurant and I.................................15
The Eye..16
Seattle Cab Stand...18
Getting a Drunk out of a Cab 20
Looking for our Own Beauty...23
How to Survive the Last Half of the Winter.............................30

Disquisitions

The Grandmother Factor..34
Our Bodies in Bed..36
For Kevin 37
Chiaroscuro..38
Under Ski Lift Chair 3...40
Disquisition on the Way to San Miguel...................................42
In a Word...43

Mark Making

Mark Making 46
Peanut Gallery..48
Trouble Shooter 50
Woman Reading, Dreaming 52
Breathing 54
Skiing with Brandon 56
Palimpsest..58

For Edith and Brandon with Love

Andante

Andante

"Spectacular women of Cali step
down from the stage and stroll
the runway out over the crowd,"
the cocaptain says. His mind's a jumbo
filled with cargo of a rich moment.

Checklists done, I taxi to and hold short
of a good gravel runway in the arctic
waiting for take off clearance.
I set the brake. Wind whips the snow.
Our world is white. We stare and wait.

He keys the intercom. "What luck,
R-O-N-ing with Miss Universe
semi-finals live in our hotel.
Beautiful women are sitting everywhere,
and they're just the sisters and mothers."

His queens come down step by step, stop,
pivot in the feast of his eyes then flow away.
The special light of the beautiful licks
along their limbs like sun and wind
on shining fields of cane waving.

No clearance. Our runway disappears
thirty yards out before the white wall of the world.
We talk. Maybe jumbos are wandering
the pole, lost again but making time.
So much having to do with speed is waiting.

Person, place, or thing, the nouns we are
mix and twist in this world of work. On verbs
of transport, we the cargo, far farrago,
soar like music, run like money.
Off Kaulapapa we rotate through surf spray

with loads of dirty leper laundry.
Off Lanai we launch three thousand
pounds of poi. We fly the Hajj.
We map the world's whales, haul her mail,
panties, and potash. We bear her roses.

But now were grounded and found. No three
a.m. forty below Gulkana ramp here.
No nurses and a doc in back attend
twin preemies splayed like skinned rabbits.
No one suctions the teabags of their lungs.

It's not Vundik Lake. No big fire, no taxiing
the Goose with backhaul trash over acres
of pike. Firecrew women don't strip clean
and swim this time. No summer midnight light,
and none flings arcs of diamonds from her hair.

For the moment we're seated at the festino lento
of the work we love. Each checklist challenge
and response seasons our concerti. Each truth
or tale plays violin and cello. This reasoning, the close
and fugal ladeedah, colors our Corelli.

"Your turn now," I'm told, "what's your story?"
Thoughts in winter pelage come clicking
like caribou to give themselves, suddenly
noticed within the wind that hides them.
And the spectacular woman of Reu

on her family's patio raises her arms,
arches her back, and shoots me a glance,
igniting the castanets, her heels, and hips.
But I begin with the washing of the elephants
and the rhino charging down the river in the dark.

Round

1492, the round world, and Barbara
Picknell kissing my lips at Christmas,
the sewing machine invented by Howe,
Miss Frasier throwing third grade
and the smell of onion at me, pulling
my hair, and Sheldon Dwyre making her stop,
beating her arms and ass
out to her car with a belt,
and my brother, who could see, sent
to the state school for the blind,
the sewing machine invented by Howe,
and Janet Miller, my beautiful Janet,
crawling out of a pup tent
at the county fair with a GI,
the blood and sperm soaking her skirt,
both laughing at her twelfth
birthday, the round world spinning
with coral islands in it,
the way hawks move and cats hold,
the reaper McCormick invented,
Barbara knocking dirt off sugar beets
down south, and me rubbing my head,
falling from trees, swimming creeks,
shooting a collie, singing slow songs,
losing my family as I step to the round world.

My Life

She walks she talks crawls on her
hugs her belly like a snake
in snow gets up tits up
an amorphous toad sits
on four bar stools at once
has no dignity
is the brown bag it comes in comes
naked to the feeders swallows the swords
hundred hotdogs one a second
flaming fats carbohydrate buckets
the chemicals crystalled metaphors
of holiness wipes a mouth
so prehensile it could climb a rope
marries midget me laughing in her laps
we swing with the moon she sings
"My life my life so short and sweet"
she hums holds it high grows
and grows amuses you
hangs from a rope by her teeth.

Before Breakup on the Chena outside Fairbanks

We flung gravel out in arcs then cut
for trees. Now shattered water answers
back. We laugh, and your hair is tender.
I cup it in my hands. Cars attack the bridge,
headlights splash, and your brown skin goes cream.

That light makes tall dogs impractical now,
bisects children, and crossing the bridge,
cuts an edge where runny noses wobble.
Last spring your dad clawed for air when ice broke
under runners and a half-breed team. Ling cod sucked

his clothes. Babies are jelly now in the walls of rabbits
and that river's wall. I think this bent fender
is Ford. That ankle, hair, hock and antler you know.
Your face is native in my hands. Owl feathers catch
in a white wall tire I can't explain. All rivers

have tires. Across the Chena a husky bitch bangs
a chain anchored in her throat. In a minute
you'll sing or cry again and rub your knees.
Look, you say, the snow when you walk on it
is like a leather wallet when you twist it.

Here a fox pinned a meal beneath his weight.
We kiss here, and our story is tracked in snow,
the way we came, running the razor water and gravel
and there your frigid angel where I explained
the blood each month and blood the first time.

Toolkit

You come with all your tools, dump brush, wrench,
hammer head, trowel, spoon, sponge, and clamp—
all dancing on our work bench. This cookie
cutter, wobbling red, is my big dumb heart.

An hour and a half north, pack ice is passing. Shorefast
on the hard dry land of water, skin boats park
ready where the shearline grinds. My hands curl cold.
What skirt's to hem, what rose to trim with this flenser?

What's to cut and culture? Another man's whale
might rise in offering, well-mannered like romance
in arched and airy rooms, to be carved into a hedge
of ribs. Must I bend and garden to your grace?

Bring on your toolkit in a cardboard box.
I will rake the heat from your hair, coax and pat,
tighten and tango. And you, dear butcher, may harpoon
please then haul in, land, and landscape thank you.

Like jack Romans lost in Gaul, we make do. We caulk,
patch and paint, refinance, lube and tune. We mother.
We father. We work on each other. The pinion
drives the bull gear, the trunion hugs the strut.

Nervous Breakdown at Neah Bay

Broke Slavs married to boats beat
the winter blues off Cape Flattery,
rolled in slop days on end, bunged
their knuckles redder on rusted gear
dragging the Shelf for sole, snapper
and cod. They cursed the green
or gray of the waves, impatient for summer
and salmon. Layered in bins, iced down
for home, the fish looked up astonished.

Pitched to the cannery dock, they brought
the only par the skipper knew.
Breaking even put the books in the black.
Grub and diesel paid for and green kids
who couldn't quit for better work
insured one more run come dawn and fog,
radar and loran to guide them where the world
pours off to Asia. A drunk local
peed on the net for laughs and luck.

Aloof and lost, she was gang banged in a fo'c'sle
bunk below the water line above the bilge.
Skiffman stuck ten dollars in her crotch
and a nickel in her nose. Cookie walked
her home so late the TV test pattern
drilled a thousand cycles through the door
to nail them in the rain.
Good byes wore a shellac look.
Sniffling till dawn, he ran the high tide beach
to catch the boat back past two cars
and a sofa soaking in the sedge.

Balkan Cleansing

Someone's cooking late left overs.
A baby's cry wanders the smoke
like a flashlight bobbing back from a crash.
Now what? That flute barely breathing.

Picture by the fire two tame snakes
swaying up in a basket. Like arms,
they conduct our cripple on the bone flute.
No lights, no TV, just music rising
like breath three plastic tents away.

We bed down on thirsty ground.
Gradually winter softens the dogs.
Tonight at ten it takes the hill.

Too soon, tomorrow rising in the cedars
alarms the light, sweaters us over
wrestling into our local color—
camouflage. Baggy sleeves
with sheep smell, scratchy wool,
bulk us out, men lucky
for the day shift. Women
roll out busy with their bowls
and fires so we can go to work.

Heading out, we shrug into our packs,
not full but weighted and floppy with rice cake,
half a can of water, and shells. We slip away
to carefully climb the clock tower
and begin another day's work
hiding from the watchers
who picture us picking off
their women at the well.

Someday the government of heaven
is coming in a baby, and this boy
clinging to my legs just might be it.
If someone lets the puppies loose,
he drops to the crawl
serious locomotion requires.
The soft things I love
are clumsy in my hands
curled from post and stone and gun.

Each dawn I go out to pee
in the rubble that used to be our street
when night lay down, and still, that melody,
like tomorrow in a story, rises again
behind my neighbor's empty barrels.
That flute, a foggy sound no sun
nor special star can burn. Sheep bells
tinkle on new ground up slope.

All night cooling on dirt, stone deaf,
too sluggish to strike, the ropy cobras
rise heathen again in a sunny basket
that should be holding bread. Our brother?
We steal him grapes and share our cheese.

The little mine in a little war that took his leg
gave him back a flute.
He drilled and whittled it a week,
this femur he thinks is his.

He nods good morning, smiles
in his daffy way and whispers
the only thing he says these days,
"I never quit. Never.
I am the river in the cedars."

Nocturne at the Institute

This black scrap from Viet Nam,
deaf paraplegic, wheels off
the basketball court with nine equal
friends. They drive their own electric
chairs.

He knows that we think the sad should not
be cruel. In the room reserved for helping them,
he writes on paper, "Tell me
just what dying is, you faggot.
ok, buddy?"

Well, I guess
it is sitting a lot, for the man who can't walk.
It is world news, for the Soldier's Home.
My liberal views on women, for women.
It is silence, for the blind.
For example, a handful of wool
landing in a pan filled with snow.
It is nothing, nothing at all,
for the cabbage down the hall.

Surviving Winter

What Makes Me Miss You

Swallowing and snow falling down does it.
Down-shifting does it, also radio late
late. And Wolfman does it, of course.
The toothache-constant time of it
does it.
I even wake up hurt.

Glassy water and weather breeding zero
zero in this bay and the next, why not,
does it, no money too, and not
a single love letter from you helping does it.
My right hand with my center fold,
my right hand with my genius does it.
My left hand with nothing,
my left hand flying a DeHavilland Beaver
on amphibious floats in a Taku wind does it.
My reverence for giving you guilt does it.
My dog getting killed does it.
The mammalian music of whales,
heartache,
and my huge plans for women.

-10

Winter in the bed.
Outside, the chalk-shriek of squalls
rings my spine with zero,
and zero rolls round
the hollow in my arms.
Dawn comes unstuck
like a tool drawer.
Outside the frosted window
God flies up in a napkin.

Coming from sleep, that surgery,
afraid to move, feeling for the cure,
the right parts missing,
I wish stoves pumped heat harder
and all my past lovers were here
cuddled under the covers
squirming slow in baby oil.
I wish one were here.
I wish I were important,
the summer sun, the number ten.

Moving Train to Cactus Transfer

The shot horse roll over
I do I do for you,
my mind on timing and technicalities
of animal fear and leather.
The high hat's to hide my face,
the strain and pride in my obscure skill.
I'm not the star you've paid to see
I'm filling in for falling
when now the whites you like are losing.

The burning man bursting through glass crash
is just how far I'll go in the glitter
to pour the points of view
right into you.
Your face now obscured by skill,
the pain whose heat you'd never believe,
whose name we want to know.
Not handsome Hepburn, beautiful Gable,
not Elangayak, Aleutian lady,
citizen called Drifting Snow.
But this, your wide-eyed eggs and bacon face in flames,
supper for the poor who watch and wait to eat.

The gangster chase into the sea car plunge
I do for fun
and the wrong I've done
to river banks and liquor stores,
a farm boy's father, librarian, Rotarian,
and the tight tight pants of a mother like yours.
The wasted faceless history of the midwest—
I do it for the plunge.

The Woman in the Big Boy Restaurant and I

I love the way she bites the O
of the donut and eats it into a C,
the way the glazing sugar sprinkles her lap
where a pink package crinkles in the heat.

I want to kiss the curlers in her hair.
I want to flex my biceps,
make payments on her station wagon,
caress her cheek with all the little holes
in it looking like a minute steak.
I want to eat her face.

I want to take my clothes off
and like a pussy cat in catnip
slither and hiss and squirm and roll all
over her four blond brats.

I want to give her an expense-paid trip for two.
I want to give her just one good night
on Diamond Head, my sports car reflecting
the glow of the distant surf,
the close pounding of the moon.

Gently I want to unbutton her fuchsia
pedal pushers and tell her it's all right.
I want to look her straight in the eye,
death's little hideout.

And then, then, I want to ease her
out of her tiger-striped bikini panties,
and before the anaconda crush of time makes us one,
I want to eat them.

The Eye
      from a drawing by Maria Molena

What, no white wink? Your one big eye
drills my face. Scream, and pencil
shut a squint. For the look we want

slap eye two against the wall, hook a nose,
fish up some lips to kiss, and hang ears
for the story you won't soon forget. Draw red hair

along the wall or scribble to catch the wind
down highway one, that one zebra stripe
curving you know where. You get the picture.

Face it, short or tall you're too much wall.
Let's rock with rack and bone. Stack the spine,
and twist the hips and brisket,

tripe and giblets, rump and chuck.
Shadow the hams, highlight the knee,
and bend the toes pushing off on a dead run,

arms pumping, original eye drilling
still. What were you, are you,
thinking? Where do you get off?

My mistake—imagination making meat
again down at the abattoir. Ditch
the body. Spit and thumb rub it

incorporeal. Lop the breast, lose
the hair to chemo. Erase the face
and brain. This trepanation mimes

the surgeon's leprous art. It moves,
it means like music, explaining nothing.
Fact is, no lens defined by lead inverts

the thought where light inquires. So,
sheet rock retina, woman window, dear
object d'art, just what are you looking at?

Seattle Cab Stand

2 x 4's of light, pine clean
and ruler straight, stud the street
where drunks and junkies lean on
lumber from the sun. Doorjams and doors
of amber air open delicious like fur.
Streets remain concrete—the sky, tin.
Five months of rain investigate
the cracks we have for something warming.

At first and Pike, that fall smell is apples
and gas. Ample harvest. Cops come
so cheap half off is free. Watercress,
kids, and kale lose their green inside
a week. They say our ex-busted chief ordered
even go lights on the corner put in jail.

The hooker on the corner wants a party—
so pretty, I tell him no. Another needs
a twenty to ease her feet, flu, and hubby's
mortgage. There are no rainbows in her pants,
and her hams don't swim curves up this block.
A gogo boy mimics meaning in this street
two ways: spread eagle and fetal squat.

At sundown a silhouette coughs,
hacks up, shoots up, shooting for the sun,
the moon, and footsteps on the moon.
Elsewhere a gargoyle gargles beer
for an evangelist, receives a leaflet,
then lifts a leg and rips a long one
over a lighted match.

Old faces look more
and more like hands your skipper had.
Statements stand out in relief:
"Something kind, you kiss—angry, hit.
When empty, you die." And the ancient white
pioneer woman who beats her bunions down
the street explains exactly what she means to no one
by swearing something awful in Duwamish.

Getting a Drunk Out of a Cab

1

It is my head in the guts
and my arm growing out of the crotch
hooking the limp legs in
and my left hand holding nearly its own
as I carry home without fare my older
brother, the body out of its mind.

The ritual spilling on the curb
with its coins, the fixing stare
and bog breath of a mastadon thawing,
the mushy fingers flexing in the rain
like gillslits pumping up a desert.
So smashed, I could tie a blue ribbon
around his cock, scot free.

Inside the weight and heat
I become the center beginning to move,
off balance enough for progress
past neon names, dancers kicking,
tits that blink on and on,
a target, a mermaid in a goblet
on a street beat by Rio or Hong Kong.
The address tied around the neck
is a hotel blurring into brick.

We move up in darkness native
to these stairs. The blind roaches memorize
chocolates old codgers leave on purpose
in the corridor. A foot hooks
the spindle railings at the landings.
I could chop it off or mother it out
without a scream or thank you.
The hibernating brain, washed clean
with wine, pisses rivers down my sleeve.

I shove the head against the doorknob
and open the lock with the necklace key,
enter, flop the body into bed. I strip him,
as I did my father once,
down the belly to the boar bear we are.

2

Of all the liquids dripping
from the holes of a man
in bed, the pastes and puddings,
the snot bubbling green
over the lip onto the lower gum
of a toothless grin whispering "more
more," of all the waxy blood in the ear,
mucus in the pubic hair,
a busted boil oozing puss—
and the rags, a handy sock, the pants cuff
I mush him clean with—of all
the meanest is the cider in the eyes.

Kindness is waking up next week
naked in a bed with complete linen
in a hotel without one woman in it.
It will be nearly daylight and already
late winter in this room. Coming to,
looking down along his life ending
in hairy legs, feet, and then a window,
forgetting scar by scar, he may wonder
when and what it was took his toe off.

I seldom dream of women now.
I dream of the limbs and liquids
of men beginning to glow in loneliness
like St. Elmo's fire on propellers
in a storm. In the midwest, my father
has checked the shed for new lambs
before eating his breakfast alone.
I feel him looking out the window
at fields of the blue drifted snow
I used to walk on
calling it the ground on Pluto.

Looking for Our Own Beauty

                I – Kevin

We moved our women out
before taking over,
then stripped the kitchen hollow
as Hello how are you.
Anything hot we made cold.
We gutted the cupboards, our knuckles raped knick
knacks off the window.
We boxed up garlic, basil,
hair curlers and a skillet
complete with grease
and deadpan about the cooking,
most of it mine.
In the living room
we junked it all on the rug.
The kitchen, the heart,
belly, and soul of the house,
echoed us in like strangers,
archeologists wondering
who lived here
and would their leaders
have liked us.

We won't know them
by what they did
but what they did it with.

For example, the lever
and wheel in this doorknob
means to come and go
be half-ready for a fight,
one hand easy
the other fisted and twisting.

Cigarette burns on linoleum
indicate they were nervous,
knew fire or speech was hot
and dropped it.

Scuff marks below this sill
reveal a witness,
too small for us,
female therefore
waiting in hard shoes.

Those dents in beige blighted walls
suggest how hard and fast truth was
between stove and sink.

The room itself,
the square tool it must have been,
makes certain their enormous need
for rhythmic music
and the beauty of children
so easy to imagine.

Now what would they say of us?
Here in the temple getting stoned
on paint fumes together, glorious,
laughing at the fall and decline
of rude beginnings and also the way you look,
doing the funky robot,
half-grown, well-muscled, and paint-speckled—
too quick with the big roller
running yellow up the wall
as we desecrate the ugliness of home.

II - Jerry Bailey

How close to spirit you are
calling at midnight to come
get you out of jail
for driving lively.

Some modern country Puck,
manly and just a little bit slick,
you salt your style with twinkies
and beer. Like most of us
you make a wife hate,
have a lucky break—two babies
and your heart in one bed,
a new lover, more paint and plainer,
waiting in another,
you on the way in a Thunderbird
sparkling like a star
roaring like a truck.

How close to spirit, you
breezing 90 down the highway,
your fingers popping to radio rock
moving smooth in God's own groove.

Soon, sirens slicing up the night,
and there's you, feeling cute:
a .38 under the seat,
a stash in the box,
the swan and stolen roses in the trunk,
and a bottle of beer in your crotch
feeling cool as the woman's hand
we've always wanted in our pants.

Getting frisked and saying, man…
Passing through the hands of the law,
it's a lean body the trooper knows,
too hard to hide a gun,
your tight black butt
slipping through his grip
like a ship's hawser
humming off a cleat.

Blowing the balloon proves it—
widens your eyes, points your ears,
says, You're drunk.

You bet a quarter you're not.
Put three of them
on the back of your hand,
flip them, catch them,
palm down one-handed
1,2,3,
in the dark.

In the glare of headlights
you walk the yellow line
to prove you can go straight
on blacktop and do,
then jump down
turn around
and make it back
double time
on the line
doing the boogaloo.

Jerry, I think of that night and wonder
how can a man live on this earth?
Here we have light, color, even fruit
but without you
no music in our moves.

Even a state trooper wonders
how close to man you are,
shined a light in your boyish face,
searching your smile
but not the car.

              III - Lou Barr

"Start a wave down your body,"
Lou Barr told me, then he rolled,
head down, rump up, black and shining
in neoprene, his fins slipping out
then down in again, smooth as a woman's
smile coming from and going back to sorrow.

His body, any man in black, going down,
the undulating dolphin kick, going green
with depth and the mystery of fish.
Arms trailing, moments, moments of grace
echoing grace of waves rolling in from Asia
and the mercury of Minamata.

This man's blunt bullet head, sensitive
to pressures, compacted with visions
of the earth crippled.
He speaks well of animals, their brilliant
colors at night, the sea lion's body
and its total control in the liquid cold.
On the speed and spiraling of their smooth moving
rides the man's pure cry for help in this world.

I hold my breath and start down
to learn, start a wave down my body,
waves swimming through my limbs still limber,
echoing out forever, good bye,

good bye, around and around the world.
We're 74 percent water,
in water and beautiful
making waves.

        IV – Father

I'm not a farmer like you, Father,
and I don't write symphonies either,
but I want to write this down:

You were stupid many times,
but it doesn't matter
because you are beautiful.

Pissy Irish bigot peasant,
bald, tough, humbled too much
by Barron, Wisconsin's bankers.
You are short, built like a badger.
Bucking bales up to the fifth tier
all day? Ah, nothing but rhythm.

When the tractor stalled in winter
in the field, you hiked out there
with bottles of ether, hand- cranking
in the cold for two weeks
before the weather warmed enough
for your kind of mechanicking to work.

One day an eagle waiting on the manure spreader,
a brown stain around the fierce beak.
Bad winters, you said,
even eagles eat shit
keeping on to kill in spring.

Once, sudden clouds, I saw you crying,
laughing, praying in tongues
to some itinerant southern preacher's
Georgia Lord for bringing the rain
that broke the drought,
both of us drenched and dancing,
barking with all the dogs.

I was in you once
where the ancient thin sting
burns for women.
I was something like one of your electrons.
You spun me silly in that sack,
orbiting, wobbling wider, whirling

around your male world, its nervous woman
you were only good to in bed,
the broken machines and eagle,
any god who'd answer, the wrench
on the rick rusting in the rain
of your wild new words.

Living alone winters later,
you moved the bed into the kitchen.
I saw you sleeping, hunched up,
covers thrown back, your cramped hands
between your legs, warmed by the softness
of your brown old leathery balls.

How to Survive the Last Half of the Winter

Grow more fur than usual.
It will fascinate you.
Be fascinated.

Depend on food.
It will heat you.
Be warm.

Keep one empty room inside you
where no one could possibly live.
It stores color for the coming flowers.

Keep your heart pumping a path
like a neighbor with a shovel.

If you are a man
take a stick and poke through the snow
for a buddy who would cook you a meal
when you need to weep and dance damn it
for the impossible beauty of your life.
Not buy you a drink
but cook you a meal
with actual avocados.
You won't find him
or he will be too cold,
and finding this out
will take time.
If you are a woman
and don't even live here
believe me it will also
snow down on your ground,
though what you should take,
what look for. . .
I don't know.
Ask me about it, though,
and this will take time,
that useful if ambivalent resource.

Bow your head slightly,
breathe evenly,
ski quietly off among the trees.
Read, drink, or pray.
Grab the table and hang on.

Learn what you can.
Let the letters come
from shy friends,
or just a note from your own endurance.
Let it say plainly
how it squats down
at a time like this
with all the bunched power in the thighs.

How it squats down,
man or woman midwife,
to lift with the thighs and buttocks clenched.
How it puts both arms down and pulls
twisting those stubborn twins
April and May
right up out of the ground
green and screaming
by the hair.

Disquisitions

The Grandmother Factor

        1

It can't be just this stepping out
into the day that gets so much like walking
and walking Neanderthal toward evening
at five through brown grass and wrappers,
nor this waiting like a vacant lot
for the ribbon cutters.

Nor even, in this case, the modern man
flying turbines all week for food,
blind on gauges in polar weather,
or nice days by the feel,
which above two thousand with others
along becomes again this walking with care
into evening and the river.

The sun and the moon—
the trouble with living,
it's so damn daily.

        2

Gramma told me that,
in a loud voice,
combing her hair into sunshine and rain
by a window with plants, her hearing aid
laid like breakfast on a plate.

Human is really an invention,
she'd say, an idea like north,
and we go around and around it
just getting there it's so flat.

She wound her beauty into a bun,
had three husbands, cared for the sick and sink,
too soon died of cancer, and now some say
a similar crab scuttles
through her womb toward you and me.
Her last boyfriend showed me how to whistle.

I look for an invention like her,
no moving parts, less wear, axe or wedge,
quick kayak sliding by north,
any spot on earth when the world is flat.

Fires are hot in the boss's turbines tonight.
Professional leaving the earth, I look down
for the right lake with her cabin light,
pinhole to the mind,
spark in the rock,
Olga, Olga.

Our Bodies in Bed

Each night our bodies silently touching—
two feed sacks budged cross-
wise in back a pickup
coming home from town.

Each night baked while we sleep,
our souls rising, breathing like yeast.
My love, we're leavened loaves,
me the wheat and you the rye.

Each night this heating up our bodies do,
this fermentation of blood and lymph
like week-old silage in the bin
that warms bare feet, makes chickens stagger
and cows go butch in the moon.

Like sea cows, slow and sexless,
the bodies roll below the surface of words.
My growing beard scrapes questions
on your arm. Your breath whistles like whales.
Your thighs answer in a criss-cross whisper.
The elbows make jokes about their masters,
and your ass has a good one on me.

Each night the unimportant eyes darken,
each face hides in a raccoon mask.
Oh, our city may smell like chocolate,
but the bodies, solving more mysteries than we,
have known for years that lunar dog is coming.

For Kevin

You'll be holding basketballs soon
one-handed from the top.
You're fifteen today and I call you
my son and (why not?) my countryman.
I get that lonely sometimes.

Technically I know just how good
your good dreams are—perhaps
your rocket wracking through space,
an older woman talking you in.

But understand my need to advise,
to give what I never knew.
Therefore, before your very eyes
in America, believe in magic:

such as this two pound stone I say
begins existing now as a grey weight
between the pink fingers of my hands.

I breathe on it once,
it burns blue and cool
to attract you.

I breathe twice,
a green river flows over my shoulders
spirals down my chest
and, looking for a future,
roars between my legs.

I breathe three times,
and it throbs as a warm white dove
between your blunt black hands.

Chiaroscuro

It's a man you see moving you call life,
my kind of dog sniffing the rich in the willows
while someone's golf goes driving out of sight.

Or the bag of your belly shifting at night with baby weight,
our boa boy in burlap. By day, the jack rabbit
jumping of it in math class, our kicking co-efficient.

It's the family the camera slows exploding on the Plain
of Jars when the strike begins. The little place
on the giant's face for David's gesture of little stone.

It's the late light he loves on Bathsheba's skin, spark
of a glance, amber shoulders, water roiling golden
and the dark place he found when he lay her down.

It's the man Breuhgel sees still moving on problem feet
beyond the frame, the skaters, and the excitable soprano
singing like poultry by the fire, scherzo petering

portamento, waving the heavy hunters home.
It's the harp in the wind, siren in the seal under ice,
that opaque ocean songs are from, clear krill they feed on.

These wooden words row your liquid language
to the sharp point where let's presume I'm missing soon.
And you will say the soul's a diaphanous gland

that can't be killed, or the fogs in fall a spider spins
forever, or the slow zoom of our son's or anyone's
regard. Show him tracks in snow, refer to wings.

Delineate dusk and dawn where the fawn resolves.
Mention mist on the Plain Of Jars, those doubtful counts.
Say stars in the lake convene arranging spring.

Bones queing back into use, life's fight for carbon—
one could go on. Or take the evening air, it's a man
you see moving, though I lay me down with the light.

Under Ski Lift Chair 3
    for Edie

In the mountain blue above us, big boys fall
through summer and shout. Chutes jerk open
to keep them decent in slow descent. Well-grounded,
we pick bunny slope blueberries where I snowplowed
slowly down once with our son skiing between my legs.
He's half-grown and gone now. Kindergarten was our best year.

The sun is a blonde kitten teasing your hair,
and our dog is sleek, gliding through grass or trees,
in and out of shadow, like love I almost want to say,
shiny and dark, coming sometimes when we call
to eat berries from our hands. Too late,
I see we are country cousins to the bear
who right here left a pile of bright blue scat.

They say a camel is a horse designed by committee
on a hot day. They say that Raven makes mischief
with light, like our boy who opens and closes the day box
on the bright design we drew for him, drawing, somehow,
ourselves less a few lumps. The least alchemy stains our hands.
They plunge down and just by feel under the cool, boiling
green of leaves, find and refine the firm nuggets, pluck
and bring forth, I almost want to say, the mountains' excrescence.

There may be yahoos above us, boys from heaven,
but there's no time. We pick and move, pick and move
in and out of shadow, working fast, to this bush
and this one and that one over there. Already the light is riding
away with dignity on its llama with soft feet, our kind of camel
for a cool day, back straight, head up, our son's brown eyes.
The day is a child who loves and leaves you.

Tomorrow, we hope, will come cupping gold
light in his hands, flinging it up into the birch leaves,
fuel for those engines in the trees.
We'll hear it falling in clumps to the yard,
you think. You place a berry, the pliant sapphire,
 jewel of his birth, on your tongue, roll it around
your sunny cheek then gnash it down.
Sweet and sour, a bright idea explodes.

Disquisition on the Way to San Miquel

No chicken bus this trip. No baby vomit,
no snot, no one staring at my watch, nor touching
(where I have it) my flimsy hair. Best of all
my bowels behave. This bus is cool and contento:
self-inflation tires, reclining seats, movies.
Charles Bronson, grown gray and puffy,
trods the boards of the globe, deeply reluctant
but fluent, shooting his guns in Spanish.

I, too, am older now by two score.
I ride with a new gang, an elegant wife
and our son, taller than I, rebel
arranging a cause, gifted and stricken with youth,
our James Dean, our Montgomery Cliff.
We look rich. We are rich.

Work some, go some, work some, go.
In Colorado Springs last week what's left of family
rendezvoused. The mountains we hiked
emptied out, stripped of their grizzlies.
From a cliff we looked east over the great plains
where homes and antelope roam the range.

We drove there packing Winchesters. We drove
and drove to the forty acre ranch of Ralph and Tho,
the new Jim Bridger and wife at their trading post
liquidating lots and pots from Indians,
skirts from Hmong. *Oma* and *Opa* were there.
Brother JD was there but no Thelma, no Louise,
and no daughter, no Becky Thatcher. Edie was there.
Edie shot skeet. We all shot skeet.

In A Word

Earth turns, I tell my dog, and at the equator
where the great engine of weather begins
all things give up their water: ocean, forest,
savannah, smokestacks, cactus, the words "come"
and "cows," workers on bikes pumping
home in their acres of skin, the lungs
of the refugees, quietly bubbling forever
in plastic tents we read about. *Come.*

In Freetown other dogs are free to sniff
and pick through trash and glass
where hands and feet can make a meal.
Heel. All dogs waddle with fat when drifts
of bodies liquify and bloat the beach.

A haze shallows the depth of field.
Goats and graves go grainy on the hill,
and that line of trees smears bluer
and bluer along the border, *Sit,*
where someone's daughter is hiding
her stubs, growing up fast, just think,
citizen, almost a woman,
using her forearms
tilting a bucket for a drink.

Fuzzy, this talking to dogs about the cause of things.
Like a Leonardo painting. *Stay.*
This blending of one thing into another
arches up and out to the poles
cooling and clouding with beautiful names,
cirrus, contrail, nimbus, mare's tail,
swirling and flaring, flying in high
across our coast like the falling falcon hands
of the TV weather lady, occluded, snappy,
pointing things out from sleeves of a gray suit.

Her story's indefinite, too, though definitely stormy
Thursday descending on us, *Down*, almost as she said
it would, broadcast machinegun staccato, *Stay*,
faint smile, in this wilderness of impossible rocks
becoming dark then blue then gauzy bright
by the weekend, *Stay*, all edge-work, a cool sfumato.

Katy, our shepherd, won't listen. *Ok*. Ears pricked
to hear subtler sound, she romps, rolls,
and runs, tongue lolling. So invigorated she is,
scooping with her nose the white rarified stuff
of exhaustion at the purest point of its cycle,
the drift of which and our northern one word for it
she has yet to catch, mouth, and make crystal clear.

Mark Making

Mark Making

I write.
The marks are small.

Even the moose who leads her calf
along our mountain road
where we begin our own long walk
presses meaning into dirt
before taking so much bulk and her calf
silently into brush.

We walk softly
and carry a small stick.

You point.
What tracks are these?

Moose.
I write, moose.

These?
Rabbit.
I write, rabbit.

Dog.
Dog.

Bear.
The wandering, wondering bear.

We turn back.
And here? And here?
You and I making our mark
walking through heaven.

Overhead a heavy scrawls
a contrail, crawling out
for Asia along the Aleutian track.

Among those islands I have seen
cats' paws walk the lee.
Once an angel's powerful wing
troubled the waters,
and I was afraid to wade.

Write big,
you say,
big as the whole road.

The light on the mountains
washes in on mist
splashing spruce,
and somewhere a thrush
is making the capes and ranges
echo bluer and bluer.

If you were the earth
because you are tiny,
and I were the sun
because I am burning,
I'd swing you like this
turning and turning
until I am done.

Together, dizzy and Dervish,
we grip the stick
and, bowing to our work,
draw letters of dirt
across the road,
expanding our theme,
as we write your words,
The Sky Is Big.

Peanut Gallery

You make walking a good cartoon—
bouncy slouching. These landscapes
you pass off as purple paper
where horizontal scribbles hold your feet.

Off-handed realist, my lunar lady,
when your moon waxes fat and turns
titian like bad butter, you whack
my dog's personal nose.

In the keystone town a riot cop stopped
your battered car turning right on red
to the supermarket's neon green bargain—
cheap chops for your parsley passion.

Coy kitten, scared as hell,
your daylights out, he let you off
with a word to the wise, then off
he roared into the big time.

We're small stuff, nits and lice
in the comb the poor have to use
important mornings. Puppies in the woods,
we go everywhere fast as we can.

Beside the boiled boot we'll later eat,
you bare your belly to the moon,
and we come kissing hard,
neck and neck, even steven.

Still, all the news, black and white,
big and bad, says life is minutely,
death vastly, personal. Saving us,
a syndicate is meeting in the dark.

In your funnies grass forever burns blue,
and your tigers quote Rousseau.
It's a zoo here, and rude monkeys gesture.
Allegedly time's elephant in pajamas

leans huge against the cage bars
reaching out for peanuts.
Rumbles croon so low only dogs hear,
and the very young. We turn, and its rare

red trumpet blasts everyone.

Trouble Shooter

Send for me when your life breaks down,
or the toilet—this morning's floppy lever,
or lover. Or cash crunch at the check out,
the clerk hating you for not being young
and your child, who is, for throwing a tantrum.

I'm your man. My eyes are clear, my hands
are clean. I'm bonded. My shoulder patch
has our company number and email.
Our logo is an angel in flight with a tool belt.
Whatever's wrong, I picture it working.

I check the technicalities of peace:
handle, lever, chain, flapper valve,
and rubber seal held tight by water's weight.
Blood shunting through the vascular bundle—
behold, the body's silly sign for love.

There should be what passes for money
in your purse and a clerk somewhere
with grace. May your child, humming a little
something from Brahms, morph to the teen
who graduates and loves you cum laude.

I scan the squawks: My kid's autistic. The tanker
captain's a drunk. My love is watered down.
An enchantment holds me vassal to an evil
suzerain. My job sucks. The stabilizer jackscrew
stripped a thread. I'm living slow death by comfort.

I fix all this. You see me with my clipboard
sketching the fit and flow, turn and torque
of one thing to another like a basketball coach
facilitating his team to synergy. I beef up
quality control, hold meetings, retrain,

and retool. Instead of milling, the water knife
with garnet dust, through pin hole and high
pressure, cuts dull steel bright. No burl, no swarf.
For toughest jobs there's roots and moon, spells
at midnight. For loss, we've naught but time's tool.

As for my own troubles I rely on the restorative
friendship of a woman. Yellow warblers
are also curative, back from Brazil singing
what spring is. Each clutch of eggs, full of promise
as a row of peas, is rich with next year's score.

When failure like a junk car settles down
on the nest of my house, I curl and dream
of the lost makers of jazz. How Horace Silver's
quintet can make you believe there is no place
like Room 608 or sister like Sister Sadie.

I follow the horns and fluid hammers out along the riff
to the final note where the beat in the heart breaks
in a bath of gritty beauty. What machining
is that? What liquid cuts like that,
cuts and cleans, cures with a perfect kerf?

Woman Reading, Dreaming

On two twenty-four the snow begins.
Doctors spin in ditches, and we're on our own.
The book is blue and bendy, best kind,
and the lady in the spine is having a baby.
Our Dear Reader, Leilani, let's say, skims pages,
ignores the chickens in the ginger patch
clucking to the mauve dawn.
It says here feedlot sheep in slush are ecru,
and the gates of life don't dilate.

At twenty thousand feet our love interest flies
home in trouble. The weather's baroque, engine's out,
and his captain is chic but dull and good, best kind.
The North Pacific is explained since God,
but on the panel the damned gauges beguile.
Double space.
The uterus clamps its bag of muscle.
We're born like toothpaste in a storm. We can't
go back. Our theme, viviparous; the plot, breach.

What's Her Name dreams she's reading on a red bed.
Trade winds enter the screen, wander
room to room like in-laws looking
for good books. Next door in air rich
with chickens nothing's louder than the Bach,
darkly perky. Engaged, head down,
ideas kick black water hard while sunroom
curtains puff chintz in a cool chartreuse.

What child comes riding? What dream?
What barging through business pidgin to the depot
on the beach of a bed? Don't argue
with a woman in transition. Sing.
Sing plywood, rebar, Portland cement, and thyroid.
Sing sternum, fingers and toes, bills of lading
from the continent. Now push, push for the lady
alone in the snow and her sister, the doctor in the ditch.

Push the airplane home on procedure
where the pros shake hands. Push corny
for the future: plumeria sweet forever in regular
weather, sheep ever steady in a windy
pastoral, and grown children you won't despise
in fading days. Bring ladders, bring hammers, music
and milk, box of blue vowels, pail of green fern.
Bring crocus and thrush. Bring soap. Kiss
your language in, and nail the daylight down.

Breathing

Waking, I swim to the surface
and hear your own soft surf of breath
breaking in the distance across the bed
where you sleep in a blonde tangle
in whose center a full day's template
takes shape.

Downstairs, too far to hear,
our son who grows each time he sleeps
becomes a man inch by inch.

Evenly, deeply, I pull in tides of air
through the sieve of the window screen
and into my nostrils, down the ribbed trunk
of trachea, branching bronchi, the lungs,
and those (What are they called?), not leaves
but alveoli,
tiny carburetors so close to the soul.

Oxygen married up in couples runs in,
or veiled as a vapor menage a trois twirls by,
hydrogen arms akimbo,
leading the cool perfume of spruce and fennel,
birch pollen, manure, bacteria, and dirt,
the scented song of thrush and finch,
this poor people's march, this diaphanous stew.

It all comes down to blood, canoeing away,
drifting limbs to the farthest trickle
in the fingers' and toes' archipelagos
where its work with carbon is crucial.

Relax,
and hot air pours out
like a drunken old man going home at night.

I rise and come to the kitchen table.
This pencil is sweet cedar. This paper,
my grade school in a field of cut hay.

My hand begins moving into words.
Even if wrong, it calls things something,
is free to say this is that.
A sock is a foot's hat.

Or thinking South, looking top down on a map,
it says we live on the right coast,
and the life we share is high
and low pressure—or else not.

It says there's treasure in a lacquer box
with an intricate scene painted on black,
a hurricane's eye inside,
or Bach's Air inside.

It says this breeze in a house of air
is the weather of love,
this breath on the leaves of our little forests
of bright red trees.

I breathe, and it all burns bright
waking me to what I am,
as air, which is many small things spinning alive,
becomes, broadly speaking, this morning
rushing in to feed my quiet fire.

Skiing With Brandon

Your name and my name, music unplayed, people
the distance here, unpackage what happens
by the Christmas of our coming, skiing, breathing.
If trees fall, you name it, without us there's no sound.
You ride inside my coat, sleeping, or peeking out,
round raccoon, so newly human. The engine
in my chest beats your brains where thought begins.

I've been thinking, and the world is round.
When hungry your mother's breasts round you out.
Born blue, you pissed, pinked, and sucked. Sculptors see
bodies in rock rounding their gray interference
and amplitude, filling full as waves in water do.
These canyon walls come hard. Snow sugars a bluff.
In cliffs no mother, no father-mirror windows you in.
Any window's a door if you're stone or light enough.

I'm not water. Still, I don't reflect.
Therefore, here is wind and names quick
on the wind, yours, mine, peregrine.
Four ravens wrangle up and tumble pizzicato
in the chrome. These hills lull and roll to rhythm,
bumbling cymbalon. Rocks and ski poles clack.
Harmony won't do. Harmony is blue.

I've been thinking your name and my name,
even music—baby rage at bedtime conducting
fists of fortissimo solos against the null.
Hear that? The soft ringing bell of the boreal owl.
"No bigger than a beer can," your granddad said,
"Can hear the pulse of a mouse in snow or ticking
of a watch." Time's the little rat in your pocket.

When I was three mother danced with a collie,
and then she danced with me. A wind like this
came up whipping its grain beyond the tractor
tacking west, crashing the owl's elm that splattered
a goat no one knew about beside the nest
and pellets and long lost tuning fork. Beware grace.
That storm creamed Bill's Café but good, set loose
the shedding adjustable lion I just now made up.

No story here but lynx, real fur and tracks, subtle
printing for the rabbit in snow who reads like snow.
Black birds debate. Imagine ravens melting,
dabs of winter night pooling in someone's song
of ending at ten. Peter Rabbit's in dutch.
Arrange a detritus disguise. Say the funny wind
in my throat is words changing to other things.

Clown them crazy for clouds. Go blank
and ravens freeze in air. Nurse the nipple
in your brain and your pacifier's the living tit
you think it is. Be common. Design otters splashing
huge in Peru. Cars, keep them honking in Kabul.
Forget the hills and heat in music and I chill.
Imagine mothers dancing. Be mistaken for everything,
and squall your name livid in my arms again.

Palimpsest

You leave for a month, first time,
and the sky with the clear skin of a boy
says nothing.

I sit down on the lawn
that I should be mowing.
The house, huge now and full of silence,
leans away
from bright bees and noisy flowers.

Rethinking,
I roll out flat
like a crumpled page
that a hand smoothes out
saving anachronisms for further study,
a palimpsest pending review.

Your voice on the phone
just dropped an octave,
and soon that baritone
will drive away wishing us well
over a light spray of gravel.

For more than a dozen years
you and your mother
splashed around every day
in the chilly lake of my life,
and I could hold you both
wild and weightless in my waves.

But now somewhere my pulse
is taking a good long walk.
And over there across the road
some bird with a red breast,
which could be a quetzal
defending the green territory of sorrow,

repeats and repeats
what could be an aria
by some gifted composer long gone
whose art, like the pyramids,
makes its point
short on ideas,
long on material.

Cloven tracks meander the yard.
The grass is flat where some pre-dawn beast
lay down like a father with his hump,
slightly exotic in dim light, moose or xebu,
to savor its cud of garden cuttings,
ruminating on noisy flowers,
oriental poppy orange explosions,
cosmos shouting pink and white,
and more subtly, sweet William,
baby's breath, and creeping phlox.
All herds graze, I suppose, on dew
and the high, two-tone tremolo
of columbine vibrating in the morning breeze.

You'll return for awhile, of course,
and the house will fill again
with your colors and gusty music.

But for now
somewhere a chainsaw is chewing up
the afternoon, and way,
way up there, those could be clouds
on a glassy lake
floating across my eyes.

I don't move.
Not Maria Callas,
not my neighbor's round robin,
not Jessye Norman,
nor all the morning mezzos
can make me shiver now.

David McElroy grew up on a farm in northern Wisconsin. He moved successively west and north by attending the universities of Minnesota, Montana, and Western Washington and taking various jobs. He has been a smokejumper, teacher in Guatemala, taxi driver, English teacher in Seattle's inner city, and currently is a pilot with over 30,000 hours flying light planes in bush Alaska from coastal southeast, Aleutians, interior, and the Arctic in support of the fishing and oil industries, forest fire control, wildlife censuses and bowhead whale surveys. He has been published in national journals and has a previous book of poems called *Making It Simple*. Winner of several grants and awards, he has given readings at various universities in the west and New York. His passions include hiking, snowshoeing, kayaking, and birding. With his wife photographer Edith Barrowclough and son Brandon, he travels widely in Alaska and the world.

www.ingramcontent.com/pod-product-compliance
Lightning Source LLC
Chambersburg PA
CBHW070551090426
42735CB00013B/3145